CPSIA information can be obtained
at www.ICGtesting.com
Printed in the USA
LVHW080955291021
701892LV00015B/201

9 781096 725992